DREAMS & HOPES OF THE BLACK ANCESTORS

Book of Poetry

MARCY T. FORPOH

SMS Write On Publishing

ISBN 978-1-7355437-6-5

This book is dedicated to ever single black person that was here before me and those ones that are here now, as well as the future ones long after I am gone.

This book serves as a springboard for black generations to be determined, courageous and to excel.

CONTENTS

CHINUA ACHEBE

A man of affluence of words
In literary ascendancy of passion.
He fought with creative swords
An ingenious catalyst of creation.

Spawning his eggs in layers of letters,
In the symmetry of synthetic fondness
Like a fire smolder.

From a ravishing gale of flames,
Beyond the glow of embers
So things started to fall apart.

When he left, no worries
But a trace of his memories.

TELL THEM

I saw a letter from a black ancestor

He wrote;
Tell them in the day they become men
That there was a country.
Tell them on the day the ask of us
That there arose a people like an eaglet
Whose feathers were plucked for a dirty ear.

If they seek answers to stains on our flag,
Show them the spot on the raising sun.
Show them the lemon tree where we hanged.

If there ask for our graves,
Tell them we have found our home in the air
Tell them we fought the land
We won the lions.

Tell them we survived the wounds
Tell them we brought home the flag.
But if they ask further,
Tell them our own brothers
Sold us for a favour before a foreign king.

Tell them that we never died on the field
We died at home in the hands of our blood.
Tell them we went like Caesar.

And in case they ask for our guns
Tell them to love but never to trust
Tell them to watch their back.
Tell them that home is deadly

And when they win the flag,
Tell them that we are bloods.
And none should be a king
Tell them these.

BLACK BOY ON THE TREE

There was a boy
Swinging on a tree.
Up and down,
Few feet from the ground
Carried by the wind.

Sad though he was
Death is seemed the worse.
On the tree he played,
The boy was very gay.
Then came the gentle breeze
Blowing with ease.

The boy laughed and smiled
He smiled and laughed
Up the tree he climbed
The branch was not enough.

So up the tree he went
And when the branches bent.
Then the boy tumbled down,
And fell from the tree
Breaking his spine.

Too much of play
Too much of laughter
If it comes today
Won't stay forever.

WHEN THE CULTURE DIES

When the culture dies,
Who is going to put dust in its eyes?
Who will be left to stand?
Who best understand
The ways of our fathers
And primitive ancestors?

When tradition dies,
How do we rely
On the origin of our heritage
Long traced from the Stone age
When civilization comes
With sophisticated norms?

When the elders are gone,
And leave us the throne

As the symbol of our past
By those who came last
How do we understand?
How to rule the land?

LAND OF BLACKS

Let's talk about the past.
About the colour of our skin
The pride of the Africans
Dwell in the pigment of our blood cottage.

Let's talk about the jungles
Of roaring lions,
And the desert of blazing sun
Upon the Sahara,
Of thousands black.

Let's talk about the negroes
The strangers of their own lands
Pariah to the natives of gluttons
That keeps the world in their pockets
And impoverish their kinsmen.

Let's talk about our lands
The lands of milk and honey
And ethnic disharmony.
Inferior to the exterior
Habitat of colonial terror.

Let's talk about our brothers
Who fed us with a scourge
Of starving hunger
Ripping the harvest meant for us
In the famine of recession.

Let's talk about the land of black
Stereotypical colour of greed
That the coastline breed
The sun shines too much,
The rain too torrential
Intense heat like human greed
Upon the terrain of its domain
Where the greedy blacks rule their world

SAVE THE BLACK CHILD

I named her before her birth
I bore her through pain and joy
At first sight, I saw my new world
Her first cry gave me peace
But never knew this peace is short
Just a few years and my Princess is slipping away
Please save the black child

Mother, she calls with happiness,
But now with tears, my heart is broken
For I am helpless to the one I live for
Please save my child
Before her birth,
I was restless and sleepless
But I will go breathless if I lose her

She holds tight onto my hand

And look deep into my eyes
With a faint voice,
She let out her question
Will I make it, mom?
This hit me beyond measure
Someone please save the black child
Before she becomes a shadow.

I know she doesn't want to leave
But her pulse is getting weaker
I don't want her to leave me memories
But we should make happy memories
That she will live to remember
Answer my prayer request
Oh saviour of all,
Please save the black child

THE MAN IN MY COUNTRY

No one wants to hear from him
Even if he cried or screamed
He was about to be eliminated
Or to be relegated

If he continues to say the truth
He won't be given a chance at the top
Especially if he is a youth
He will just be dismissed or stopped

The man in my father's land
That holds all the pledges
And vows in his right hand
If fortunately was selected
He will just be kept or muted

The man with the love of my country

With great ambition,
That love not only his territory
Was called a pollution to the nation

The man in my nation can't even utter a word
Because, they said, he holds a sword
The sword is not against the county,
But their self interest
That is while the man in my country was muted.

THE AFRICAN STORY

Africa my continent
A place rooted in creativity.
We are the enigma that many nations
Still hunger to unravel.
Africa is beauty yet untapped.

It is creativity wrapped in vestures of fine linen.
Africa is a world ready for discovery.

We have heard the stories from other lands.
We have turned captivated eyes
To watch the moving movies of the western world.
We have been held spellbound by tales from the TV screen.
We hunger to tell our own stories.

I am a writer, Pen poised
To tell the world of the beauty
Hidden in the history books
Of the African heritage.

I hunger to tell the world the African stories of warriors
Of feasts of plenty and people of great resource
Who create from the little resources they hold.

I want the world to hear The African voice
To dance to the beat of the samba drums
To hear about the lobola
That announces a bride to her home
To listen to the sound of the waterfalls
In the Nigerian Northern regions,
To discover the thrills of The Mambilla Plateau
And to luxuriate in the diversity
Of the numerous African tribes,
That embrace unity.

Like Martin Luther King
I have a dream
That the whole world will one day
Luxuriate in the rhythm of the African song.
I dream of the greatness of the African continent.
My pen is there to rewrite the African tale.
I sit here, armed
With my compendium of African history.

I will send it to every part of the world
For my pen must make an impact
The African Song must not lose its melody.

TEARS IN THE LAND

The moon has turned red
Pregnant by blood of the dead
The sun now stands still
For its grief has no pill.

What a gloomy day!
While we watch and play,
We become prey to our Predator,
'Rip off their skin' says the Dictator.

Without mercy,
Without pity,
The shooting
The killing

Soldiers trained for war
Now parade in Parlour

Judges armed with law
Now lie on the floor.

Have they not seen?
Blood spilling on the scene?
What have we done wrong?
In singing our Father's Song.

How do we build a nation?
With violence and corruption?
will "peace reign'
When we spill blood like rain?

Dear Nation! I weep for thee!
No more broken shall thou be
For our tears have gone to heaven
And we shall not be forsaken.

I AM A FIGHTER

How can I survive in a world of the fittest?
How can I live when I am the fit-less?
I live among wild beasts,
Who use men for their feasts.

I am surrounded by hunters with deadly fangs
Who speak jargon and unknown slangs.
They say "You must be brave"
To survive in a lion's cave.

Like a dwarf amidst the giant
To survive, I must be gallant,
In this world of woes and strive
I must be brave to survive.

Like a woman in the theatre
Pushing hard to save her daughter

Without giving up in the centre,
So I choose to be a fighter.

I can never bow low
No matter the numbers of arrow
I have to cross the border
I must fight till I conquer.

Our children are being hunted
The weak are always molested
The land is filled with hunters
To save the weak, I must be a fighter.

I fight with my bare palms
Not with chariots or iron arms
I fight for the weak and mild
I fight to save the lost child

I fight for the broken
I raise the downtrodden,
Join me in this fight
Together, we can win the fight.

THE MASK

Authorism!
Literally pseudonym
Secret society!
Known for hidden identity.

An abomination
Has befallen this generation
A thing of moonlight
Is seen in broad day light.

Moon night ghosts
Have become holy ghosts
Our streets are now paraded
By masking masquerade.

Beauty is no more beheld
Beauty is now inhaled

The face of an angel
Is now bathed with masking gel.

Today, you can identify
Faces of infant butterfly
But that of our maiden
Is now measly hidden.

God's own image; now turns idol
Beautiful creatures; now become dull
Beautiful faces
Have turned faeces.

The mask has made us slaves
Sending our youth to early graves
If I may ask,
What happens if you don't mask?

AN APOLOGY

I am sorry
The other day, we sat together
We talked about a better society
But I didn't tell you about its builder.

I am sorry
I know I have done wrong
For keeping this apology,
Far too long.

I talk about politics
Entertainment and gossips
But I never talk about the saving grace
And how you can win the heavenly race.

Pardon my manners
For not telling you about our heavenly father

Whose love is for all sinners
That they may escape eternal danger.

I beg your pardon
Cause there's no reason
You should spend eternity in prison
After the Saviour died and has risen,

Please forgive me
For shying away from proclaiming,
The event on Calvary
How Christ died to set you free.

Be kind to forgive
If I've never told you to believe
In him who went to prepare
A place for us to live.

He came for your sins to bear
And this message he wants you to share
He can mend and rescue you
Believe; Repent; Baptize; you must do.

TEARS OF A LOST CHILD

In her search for job
Her head was cut off
What a world of madness
Men drinking the wine of wickedness.

An innocent child,
Devoured in the wild,
Raped and molested
Buried and her body fusted.

My heart is heavy
The land is bloody
My body is weak
My lips can't speak.

Society all watching
Government doing nothing

Innocent souls are dying
Leaving family all mourning.

Leaders of tomorrow
Now victims of sorrow
And for how long
Will you continue this wrong.

RIP is not for the dead
For the dead have no bed
Weeping is all we have
Like a cow who lost her calf.

We all watch our youths die,
And all we do is cry
But solace in God, we must take
For He alone does not forsake.

THE BROKEN WORLD

Once there was a world
With peace within its wall
But men in their quest
For blood to quench their thirst

Brought darkness in this world
Causing the world to be broken
With all its peace now forgotten

A world of darkness;
Violence and wickedness
A world of manipulation;
Bribery and corruption

A world of alcoholism;
Favouritism and cultism
A world of affliction;

Brutality and persecution

A world of suffering;
Killing and kidnapping
A world of prostitution;
Betrayal and deception

A world of violence;
Hypocrisy and pretence
A world of addiction;
Greediness and oppression

A world of injustice;
Hatred and lack of peace
A world of depression;
Unfaithfulness and rejection

But there is a perfect world
Whose king is our Lord
Where love and peace abide
No danger or troubles hide

A world that shines so bright
Where there is no day or night
A world of eternal life
Where there is no war or strife

A world ruled by Christ
And devoid of all crises

A world of love and care
Where evil is brought to bare

This is the world I long to be
Where there is no misery
A world of happiness
Devoid of brokenness

NEVER WRITE ME A TRIBUTE

Rest in peace is never for the dead
The dead do not rest, for they have no bed
Rest in peace is for those alive
Who needs peace in order to survive.

I know someday I will surely die
And when I die never ask God why
This is because you never cared
A cup of rice you never shared.

When I was alive; roaming the street,
You never cared about what I'll eat
When I was hungry; in need of food
You were too busy looking for 'wood'.

What now is the need of your tears?
When I've been starving all these years?

Why now sing me a tribute song?
When you kept saying I was wrong?

Now I'm dead, you want to show you really care
When I was alive, you were never there
So if I die never say good of me
Cause while alive, you only said ill of me.

Never write me a tribute when I'm dead
Never place a flower on my bed
If I die never write me a tribute
When a cup of rice you refuse to contribute.

WHY WARS

We won't find peace
Under the shadows of war.

We won't fetch love
In the pool of the bloodshed.

We suffer our children
When we kill
When our wisdom starts to fail,
Let us all cry to God above
He knows us well.

And when the poor feel hurt,
Heavens cry too
Why wars?

Are we not brothers?
One... under the sun
Why do people destroy,
What God created?

The life so pure
And the freedom God pours,
He's love in the air
And the forgiveness he gives

All seems in vain
By the art of the men

Why do we hate?
Are we not the children of the world?
Look Heavens mourns when we hate
And when we defile the holy land.

Why do we destroy our world and the animals,
That God gave us to look after
By our swords and the guns at war?

With our children's future in ruin
We celebrate the glory of war,
With no direction or destiny
We stand proudly, very tall.

When we kill our brothers,

And when send soldiers to war.
Why wars?

OUR TEARS

We shine daily, yet we are the darkest stars in life.
Our sitting parts suffer in church
Yet our minds are graves
Holding the nature of evil, the sin.

Bushes make the youths to be in-a-cent of freedom (innocent) while they smoke,
Commit murder, kidnap and dine
In cultism and in sacred stealing.

In church, we push the Words of a book
To another realm, no more immoral things
Or sin that exists,
Preachers talk prosperity and blessings,
Blessing the Yahoo-minded to be fruitful
In the works of their hands
So he could have some seeds.

Where is the truth again?
Lies flood the globe, and they're regarded
As the truth in any pot they're found.
For its taste is sweet, today,
But how about the tomorrow's taste?

Our schools today are the printed copies
Of sin; mal-practices in exam, bribery of lecturers for grades,
And indecent dressing birthing prostitution,
How can one get to the roof,
When the ladder is pieced?

Sin has become like air, it's everywhere
So everyone is righteous
And the righteous are felling guilty
For being righteous,
Oh! ..... Oh!
May my tears never flow for the evil alone,
But for joy at last.

REBIRTH

I have a greater course
A dream of a thousand men
But life dealt me a blow
I almost did not recover.

It took me all I got;
It took me my dreams
It took me investments
My passion alone kept me believing.

Slowly, I found my way back to the creative world
Summoned my pen
Ordered my sheets
Commanded my lamp.

Guys, it time to create
All the night we worked

Traveling far beyond
To reclaim the lost treasure; My Write.

We fought thoughts
We challenge the laws of the universe
We broke nature's pride
We rode on horse backs past the sacred mysteries
We questioned the Oracle of existence
All the night we battle
Our swords were hungry to kill.

By dawn, the trumpet sounded loud
We won, victory was reclaimed
This is my Rebirth

HELL ON EARTH

I see flames, smoke, fire
The sound of explosive everywhere
Man conscienceless shooting his fellow men
See children running
Mothers in tears,
Fathers are helpless
They cried, and their tears never dropped
Only their souls can be heard
Oh, woe to the Earth
The son of perdition has come
The destroyer, master of evil.

The sun has been turned into darkness
The moon has lost her light
Death is far, and the earth bleeds
The oppressor is within thy borders

He whom the good book spoke of
As the terror of humanity
Brace yourselves, mankind
For darkness is in thy midst
Thick darkness is within thy borders.

I see gnashing of teeth
Doubled afflictions and sorrows
Sickness plaguing humanity
I see humanity being divided
Liberty is a prohibition in that system
For there is a price to do your will
I see humanity enslaved.

Regrets run wide
Terror is upon the face of the Earth
The whole creation looks on
As the oppressor's reign of anguish begins
Can humanity be saved?
Is there a hope for the lost?
Perhaps, we should have listened
When the good book spoke
We should have inclined our ears
To Heaven's voice
Where do we go from here?
To whom shall we run too?
Light is within thee
Search it! Find it!
Make hay, for eternity, calls out,

And thy future seeks rest
From this world of corruption.

Humanity! Humans fight for yourself
Fight with all you can
Fight with your tears, your strength
Fight with your blood, your life
Fight, oh fight, fight this
For you will seek death and never find
When I spoke of the law coming
To alter the cycle of existence
Which is only a matter of time situation
The hours of darkness is fast coming
For he seeks disciples for his end.

The one who bled and died for you
Weeps continually at how the mighty have fallen
How could you?
I bled for you; he says!
My cross hangs on Calvary's tree for you, He says!
Mercy still stands sure
Forgiveness is certain
Come back oh sinner, Awaken oh sleeping giant,
The reign of terror is upon us
We must fight to stay afloat.

The humanity I lived for
The humanity I have fought for and build
The humanity I died for and justified

Who did this to her!
I cry not for the present now
But for the age of humanity in that dark hour,
But I will keep praying for you
That His mercy fetches you.

AFRICAN CHILD

The bird has a nest
The ants, at times, rest
Animals have their cover
Their skin is their life saver.

The hibiscus work not
Rabbits never lack a nut
The fishes play all day
They eat without pay.

Yet here I am, a boy
Day I work the soil,
With just a wish that I live
How many night on a cave,
And days without food?
Our seeds are gone in the flood.

Our land is rich but we hunger
The bullet has taken the scepter,
We live with no hope for morrow
For what has morrow but sorrow.

From my young age,
I have faced sword edge
I have known damage
Scars that refuse to heal
I have known that pain is real
The spears are killing our zeal

Who will save us from this jungle
Who will save us from this struggle
Our strength is falling
Our hope is dying.

But we know
After this snow
The sun will show
We will rise from below

Yes, we will survive
We will live
Our name printed in history
This will be our story
A new Africa
A new people
A new heritage.

BACKTRACK TO THE GODS

I would like to visit the gods of my ancestors.
The ancestors of my land.
The spirits of my chiefs
The spirits of our long dead elders.

I want to pump them about a few big things,
About the importance of the talking drum and the folk tales
The moon days and the stream bathing.

I would like to quiz them about life
How they managed to live in peace and harmony
What caused them to fight.
Why they chose good leaders and gave
Power to the weak, evil ones.

I want to interrogate the elders

The spirits of their dead bodies
To tell me how mud homes were strong
How families were united
How jealous became a culture
Why hatred is affecting us today.

For sure, I will be aggressive but formal.
Of course, to the gods
Why they gave way to pain
Which dry the smiles of our children
Harden our son's hearts with grief
Which lured our girls' souls
To be fascinated to pain.

For sure I know, I won't get the answers
Neither will I reach them nor talk to them
For the elders are asleep
The gods are dead. We are lost.

ECHOS OF A DEPRESSED CHILD

I am only ten years of age.
All I know is study, eat and watch.
Watch the plays of the days that
Bring forth nothing but sadness.

I am only a child who is afraid of
The unknown future.
The future that haunts me each
And every day, like the darkest past.
I live in insecurity, neglect, pain and hurt!
Hurt from the abuse, I receive each
And every day.

I am only a child who has been
Drowned in depression.
No one harkens to my stories!
The hurtful stories I birth out from

My broken heart through my mouth.
Only my ears hear my stories.

My mother, she's busy with her career,
Job and shopping.
My father, he's busy with his company,
Competitors and expenses.
They think, the only best interest of me
Is cartoon, books and school.
So as long I eat and sleep, to them
That is just cool.

But that's just not all I want.
I want a mother who is a real mother.
I want a father who is a real father.
I want guidance, direction and above all
I want discipline.

I don't know what to do

PRAYER FOR AFRICA

To you alone, who are more humble than a dove
And clever than a snake,
We, like Joseph's brother's sheaves
We bow down in worship of you.

Like the larks warbler to the
Beauty of the trees and flowers,
We sing Hosanna, Hosanna to thee, OH Lord.

From the purest part of our darkened hearts,
We come to worship, adore, praise and seek you.
Showing reverence to you, Lord.
Listen to our prayer.

With our limited knowledge,
We assume that the pillars of the World are in shake.
We fear like snakes in the depth of water,

Are afraid of the eagle's catch.
The darkest night has befallen on us.
It's piling us like oranges in a bedsides hand.

Our fate is like that of Noah's flood.
Sickness keeps knocking on our doors.
The air is polluted with sickness,
The pandemic is on strike.

Once again, the world's womb has given
Birth to foolish, greedy and corrupted leaders.
Those who feed on our hardest toil.
They share not our sweet brought by our sweat.
They are greedy!!
Their homes are walled with hot bullets.
We are like people who are chased
From the garden of Eden.
Yet ruled by those who chased us.

The land is average, with average homes

And we, the average people, live there.
Yet we have failed to train our children with average morals.

Rather, with merit, they qualify
To dance to Jezebel tunes.
To become prodigal sons and daughters.

Homes fall like the walls of Jericho.
Divorce is a game of dice,
The married know how to play it well.
Fighting is now a sign of love.
Maturity is little hate.
Love is defined on the basis of abuse.
Smiles are no longer warm,
Because as for now, behind every smile
Lies an act of betrayal.

Our schools are led by a group of philosophies.
Those who teach us how to fish from the sky.
For the fact that water pours from the sky,
They think fish is found there.

Knowledge is limited,
So as long as one remembers
How to boil water is educated. Wisdom is rated by How
much you know
And quote the words of a world's legend.

The world is a set; the Church is its subset.
Where milk is mixed with eggs for deliverance.
Where pastors are paid to preach.
Where prophets are respected by people's wives,
Then they do to their husbands.

Dear God, like flogs in a dry Land
We long to be in you "River of life."

Like birds' eggs,
We long to be under your shadow.
The world is bleeding.

Forgive us our sins, God, as we also forgive those
Who sin against us.
Even those who feel we are only animals.
Those who come with liquor to us in
Exchange for our lands.
Those who take our resources.
Those devils who take power when we are studying,
Working and watching TV.
Those we call until anders.

Forgive us, for we also count their sins,
When ours are more.
For we also practice fornication, adultery
And kill each other,
Forgive us Lord.

With respect to your throne, we pray.
That God you come to our aid.
Give us leaders with a heart.
Give us the spirit of love.

BEYOND DESIRABLE CHOICES

Nothing crosses my thoughts seems so logical.
My mind is without a common call.
At a time when, orange turns blue.
I settle into depression without a clue.

Naked and dangling, will I walk in public.
I've lost my sanity even when I am catholic.
All l achieved drooling under the carpet.
Lunacy and madness have me for a target.

With a sad feeling that feels so comforting.
Deep within my oblong,
I fall for this ugliness so compelling.
As I start my long walk to the doomed Isle.
Kinky and greasy will my hair be, so I smell.

Sad to know, mine is a psychopathic

Diary of vicissitude.
I heard them say I am a basket case
With an ugly attitude.
Just laugh and take no offense,
I am beyond desirable choices.

THE BEAST SEEMS SWEET BUT WHAT'S WRONG WITH THE ANGEL

If I had a verdict to appease the gods,
With a thousand words, my words would be romantic.

A basket case full of anxiety,
The mind is like a garage
Bending not to proprietary.
Deep in the Atlantic, an ocean of reason,

A feeling of warmth.
Her eyes a glance of rare moral feeble snare,
An attack to the hidden chambers.

A stroke of goodness,
Drums of the chest beating beautifully
Unto the unspoken sensation.
I search for love like a village chicken,

Searching for it's meal.

I feel mine is most and still hard to find.
I see a similar feeling.
These feelings are to the latter.
I chose to be found by my heart keeper,
A myth upon solving a basket case.
But who shall be all I wonder. Can I be found?

I have learnt to fish but all that I catch
I cannot dine on.
Even with wine the taste is untamed,
A near commit to a vomit.
Should I say I am a lazy hunter
Who only hunts the unhealthy deer?

Is it I that does the failing or my eyes
That trick my heart for deep diving?
The uncertainties within are overwhelmed
To be digested. A need for justice,
But who will get a lawyer?

The water is high. Motions of life are only from I,
And I am slowly seeing the water rise to my face.
Should I swim for it or choose to drown till the noise Is off
a switch put down?

I see the feeling why I can't get it.

The gates seem to be open,
Yet my feet don't seem to move an inch.
The pain of getting the wrong lover
Is a pinch ticklish o the confusion.

BLACK SMOKE

On the inside flames are all consuming me
A fire is burning while I try to break free
Clouds of black smoke are engulfing me
I need some air. I'm gasping. I can't breathe.

Someone please put out the flame
It has nearly rotted to my brain
I can't see clearly, the smoke has blocked my sight
I only see the darkness. I no longer see the light.

I can't figure out how to stop this burn
Someone please save me from this wretched place
Freedom is something I have too long yearned
My soul's been tortured by your twisted knife.

I need to break free from the chains that bind me
But I've lost the key, Can someone please find me

Soon there will be nothing left of me,
But the cloud of smoke
All the fire that is inside me
Is now causing me to choke.

I am slowly dying, my air you've taken away
Smoke you need to leave, it's time to go,
You cannot stay . Gasping and coughing,
I want to breathe today
Please remove the dark cloud, I beg and I pray.

FOSTER KID

A nightstand with a single bed
A little room for me to rest
Where I laid down my weary head,
Hugging my arms across my chest.

My mother had to go away
To get sober and find recovery
A couple of foster parents took us in
I was so angry for my nap at 1pm.

No naps for her anymore, she's four!
My mom had told them, I remember,
Coffee ice cream for the first time.

A visit with my father every second weekend
Out for a burger and fries at McDicks
Weird these memories

The ones that stick.

I remember the welding,
My foster "Dad" had done
Sparks flying and the covering on his face
A chained link fence to keep
The cows and bulls in place.

The day we couldn't leave the shed
The bull was too close to the door, he said.
Oh, the memories I kept
Some I'd hidden away
A wall I put up to hide the pain
And stuck in my mind, they stayed.

The time went by so very slow
Missed you, mom more than you know
Now I've gotten older
And never wished my children
To go through any of these things
Or experience any of the pain that it did bring.

It seems I've made mistakes of my own
But, all I can do now is continue to grow.

MY ESCAPE

In my hand, I hold this book
Reading has taken me away
An ocean view, I overlook
As the waves wash me astray.

Take me into the vast ocean,
And cast me out to sea
While I read poetry in motion,
I feel completely free.

So thankful for my escape
Within this magical world,
Waves, they crash and break
As my heart becomes unfurled.

Deeply breathing in the air,

A cool breeze comes over me
Lets imagination flare
And brings me to one knee.

NIGHT TIME DEPRESSION

She hated the night
She longed to be free
She had lost her fight
So dark she couldn't see.

Her eyes were welling up
With tears streaming down her face,
In her sadness, she was stuck
Feeling completely out of place.

When she laid down to rest,
And closed her eyes to go sleep
Panic looming in her chest
Inner pain so very deep.

Nightmares go away,
And let this poor girl sleep

Every night she'd pray
And to herself, she'd weep.

The monster in her sleep
He was so very real
All her secrets he did keep
As she tried so hard to heal.

One day, the tears she cries
Will bring peace upon her heart
And all her feelings not denied
Will become her brand new start.

MORE TIME

Memories of yesterday
So many moments, they did pass
Quickly came, then faded away
Slipping through the hourglass.

No matter how hard we try
The sand slips through the cracks
These moments we can't deny
These times we won't get back.

We heard your laugh inside our mind
We saw your smile with eyes closed
We felt your presence lost in time
While we tried to stay composed.

We always thought we'd have more time
To see you and hear your voice

Missed moments and memories chime
We forgot we had no choice.

We don't decide the final grain of sand
Cherish them while they're still here
When the clock does turn its final hand,
We're left wishing they're still near.

THE GIFT

When you're empty and depressed,
When anxiety builds inside your chest,
When nothing's right and all's a mess
When life keeps giving you more tests.

When you have nothing left to cry
When all your tears have now run dry,
When all alone, you sit and sigh
When time does go too fastly by.

It is time to open up your eyes
Rain it falls before blue skies
It time to listen to your heart
A calm will make the storm depart.

All your trials and your tests
All your troubles and your fear

Will only teach you that you're blessed
When they begin to disappear.

We do not get to choose this life
Nor the troubles that come with
Even through our pain and strife,
We can choose to see the gift.

WE ALL

We all wonder who we are
Some days we just don't know
We all have looked upon a star
On days, strong wind did blow.

We all have stood beneath a tree
To watch clouds form in the sky
We've all been down on bended knee
And to someone, we have cried.

We all walk this path through life
Many different roads we take
All of us are human
Shed red blood, and our hearts break.

This world of ours it needs repair
So many of us we need to change

People hurting and in despair
While others' hearts need rearranged.

Next time you look up at the sky
Remember, you are not alone
Someone else is looking too
In the place that they call home.

BLACK SHE

She writes like her soul set fire to her heart
And her pen is extinguishing the flames.
She sings like betrayal, left her blood frozen
And her voice is thawing her veins.

She plays guitar like the strings are her disgraces,
And her nails scratch away the shame.
She dances like plague rats, blight her psyche
And her feet stamp away the pain.

She lashes out like crazed hornets
Haunt her spirit and her hands
Are weapons of rage.
She cries, like life left her broken
And her tears are warm healing rain.

She prays like her wings,
Were stolen and her pleas
Will grant her flight again.

THE PHENOMENA

The feeling of holding one's head up
For a flag of all free!
Wailing like horns across the Horn of Africa,
To the Soyinka of Africa!
Don John of Austria is riding to the sea.

Poets are on their knees
Holding the hilt of their weapon,
Mightier than swords, they say
One who cries: "Fall is the news I brought"
Cos, his conquer and to save
With his pen has changed
To discouragement and fear.

This is the tale of the man,
Who heard a word in the night, while sleeping?
Or in the midday, while walking

Or in the morning while taking bath
And decide to show the path of righteousness
To this cave, we called world.

A poet's lip was his pen
An angry man was he
The blood beats in his ear
The blood ran hot on his head
And that's the feeling,
While a poet trying to give their best
To change this world.

All they crave for is being minded
For people to read their pieces as a book of yore
And the runes that were written of old
On papers, his under the moor.

Real poets are to be cleansed
For they're one of the pillars that
Promote peace in the universe.

MY DREAMS

Dying, slowly fading into thin air,
Like a ghost, twisting and turning,
Writhing and wreathing,
Sporadically falling into the valley of
Broken dreams.

Forgotten, like garbage thrown into the
Lowest part of the subconscious mind,
Scampering and stammering,
Breaking and bending,
Like the softest metal on the face of the earth.

But alas, Persistence,
Unyielding like a mountain that reaches
For the face of the sky
Slowly searing the farthest reach of my soul:
Growing and glowing,

Fuming and flaming,
Like a wind strand of passionate desire.

Awakening, like a young hatching,
Breaking through the shell of dead hopes,
Fueled by this fragile fire,
Stepping out of deep mire
Onto a greener field.

Graciously, lifting this sombre tune,
Off my heavy soul;
Jingling and dangling,
Glitching and glittering,
Like a precious gem once brought to light.

Aye, my dreams are so alive.

POETS

Poets come without the hype
A vision sure of best intent
And field their craft in static type
A verse or two and they're content.

For poets often like surprise
The sweetest line, a turn of phrase
Avoiding cliched compromise
And uphold truth to end of days.

A vision woven without toil
A legend told of times long past
The caldron black is on the boil
The stage is set; the spell is cast.

For ancient ones have thus foretold,
The place in which the prophets lay

Fast concealed by men of old
And keeps us guessing to this day.

So having set her words in stone
The poet leaves without a sound
She acts by stealth, yet not alone
Her allies tightly gathered round.

To ponder what the poet say
As life springs from eternal youth,
The seed of knowledge has it's way
And bear the fruit of sacred truth.

WHEN THE WAR IS OVER

When the rain of bullets freeze,
And the thunder of bombs calm,
When the vulture's bellies are full,
Never to eat more carcasses,
We'll sing songs of victory and peace.

When the hailstones of anger and hatred,
Soon melt down and ease,
The red flood will wash all sins,
And snow peace fills our land again,
We'll sing the songs of victory and peace.

Ocean ripples will calm and a cool breeze takes over,
We'll come back home to my birthplace,
Meet childhood friends and neighbors,
The gods would have listened,
We'll sing the songs of victory and peace.

The dove will return with olive leaf,
Rainbow will cast it's amber colors on the sky,
The birds will hum choruses,
I yearn to see peace restored again,
We'll sing the songs of victory and peace.

WELCOME TO KENYA

Welcome to the land of tranquility,
Shielded and defended by justice,
Prayerful and God-fearing people,
You'll be warmly welcomed by great serenity,
Land gifted in athletics and rich culture.

Enjoy the stay at Diani beach,
World's most peaceful and cool place to be,
Dance to the drumbeats of Giriama dances,
Listen to the melodious voices of coast ladies,
Very impressive dressing with shukas.

An abode of the big five animals,
A sanctuary of eye captivating flamingos,
The glance of white rhinos and rare giraffe species,
Never miss you at Masai mara park,
Yes! Seasonal walk of wild beasts,

One of world's wonders.

We are the placenta of River Nile,
Crafted by escapements of the great Rift valley,
Storing the history of the first man,
Never forget great delicacies of nyama choma,
The soil that birth Jomo Kenyatta.

LOST PRIDE

I am a girl, crafted by the Master,
With curved and smooth lips,
A beautiful flower in Africa,
With attractive blooms of petals.

My firm pointed oranges,
Attracted many suitors,
Many who craved for me,
Tame princess to a queen,
Their intentions were poisoned honey.

I fell in this den,
Of fierce lions and hyenas,
Moved by ego and greed,
I was tarnished and made filthy.
Dignity lost and now a battle of buffalos.

Those who promised heaven took me to hell,
Sired children they couldn't feed,
Turned my house into a brothel,
I'm a definition of shame,
A reality of rape and mutilation.

CLIMATE CHANGE

Lights go off,
Buttons shutter and clothes yell,
Charged bodies get close and attract,
Seconds, minutes, and hours,
The time spent creating a disaster.

Children germinate in a cluster than grass,
More food is needed for the population,
Earth becomes limited for settlement,
Lives are encroached and things start to change,
We've bred what we face now.

Selfishness has grown in our hearts,
The earth we've unclothe and left naked,
Leaving our fertile soil barren,
Mother nature's anger heating,
Who's to blame now.

We need conservation agriculture,
Safe fuel that pollutes not our environment,
Save the extremes before we get there,
We can do it better for the next generation,
Or else we'll drown in this poison we're cooking.

GOODBYE BOBBY S. GEORGE

A loner is gone, one who kept everything on a low
Heaven needs visiting hours because
I got someone I need to talk to.

You never said I'm leaving
You never said goodbye
You were gone before I knew it
And only God knew why.

A million times I needed you
A million times I cried
If love alone could have saved you
You never would've died.

Thanks for the million times
You kept me on your shoulders
When paying bills from my end was maybe

Thanks for those days
When the only thing we had were big dreams.
So we spoke less and think louder.

In life I loved you dearly
In death I love you still
In my heart you hold a place
That no one could ever fill

It broke my heart to lose you
But you didn't go alone
A part of me went with

TILL IT'S TOO LATE

Finally, they've brought him
Those sweet-smelling roses
But he can't smell them.
Dead people have dead noses.

Finally, his well-to-do families
Have visited his place
And wanna pay for all the funeral bills
But it'd have been more helpful
If they showed up at his sick bed
And brought her pills.

Finally, everyone is a poet, sugarcoating.
Eulogies as sweet as honeycomb
But dead people have dead ears.
He'd have smiled in his tomb.

Finally, everyone is present at
The house that echoed with his cries.
He'd have been glad, but he can't see.
Dead people have dead eyes.

Finally, he has six people:
Geared to carry her funerary crate.
No one ever wanted to lift him up
When he was down till it's too late.

LOST BUT FOUND

Beneath my figure lie my bowl of tears,
My reflection seems sad with a great deal of stress,
Drop by drop, the ripple of tears thickens.
To the brim, it rises through my teary scenes.

To the ceiling, I stare for my oceans to dry,
Not much of a difference though I had to try,
To the brim are my tanks and overflowing at will.
The weakness within is depression so real.

Oblivious is the sight out my numerous windows,
Arrows of pain everywhere shot my killer bows,
Either the devil or the deep blue sea,
Mine are the choices for me to see.

With confusion my own and nowhere to go,
My tanks dried down with ideas on a low,

No way seems safe, but quitting is dumb,
Be creative Mama Liberia, don't feel so numb!

Up hops my pen to land on a book,
Weird explains the shock of my every look.
Drained are oceans at the sight of awe,
How possible is this before I reach for door?

Skipped to when I grinned at my pen,
Away from when I was thrown
To the den for 14 years.
Small is my circle, but I still breath
Out my black breath.
Yes, I hail from the black womb,
The echo of the black voice, black dreams,
Black thoughts. Rebirth of the black ark
Mother land Liberia found me when my questions were
WHEN!

UNDERRATED

Arrogant qualifies the name I am called,
Too much pride, they say with nothing to afford,
Remarks through air for me to endure.
To stop not needed for me, to be sure.

On and on I give my best,
Mocked with brokenness, I'm told to rest.
Contaminated became my dreams
With laughter and sneer,
Walked on I did with pain at heart so hard to bear.

Air so light encourage heavy trees to dance,
Hard for me, with lions all around ready to pounce,
Growls heard loud with every effort I make,
Focused still amidst the tears and heartache.

Poets are a result of idleness I heard,

Unknown are the mumbles with
Negativities in their head,
Echoes of "Get a job" haunt my every sleep,
Pain of insults truly cut so deep.

Overrated, they chant along with my name,
United in hate makes them all the same,
Hard it is for them to even give a break,
On a cliff's edge, I stand with my talent at stake.

Disturb not your head, for these lines are smooth,
Hate is constant no matter how good the root,
All I'm called, I embrace with pride,
Amidst being so underrated, I'm enjoying my ride.

WHAT MAKES YOU BETTER

Being broke is not by choice,
Judge not the tides of all coins,
Unfair is life, so row your boat,
Not all alive have a colorful coat.

What level are you before you point?
Who made you a prophet with rights to anoint?
Judge not a race, you know not its end,
Your straightness could one day end up with a bend.

Vanity is wealth, so learn not to oppress,
Be careful with those you choose to depress,
Your wealthy existence should stir up no tears,
Tables do turn with karma, serving your shares.

Oh, humans heed not to the voice of arrogance,
Look down on no one while having the chance.

Tomorrow is like a scroll with unwritten verses.
Your reject today could end up signing your passes.

Humility is key even at your strongest.
Unknown is how arrogance is easy to digest,
The pride of a peacock makes it not a top dog,
Your ridicule of others makes you nothing but a clog.

Paddle your canoe and live longer.
What others go through is not for you to bother,
What makes you better than those you taunt?
Beware! For like ghosts, they'd always come back to haunt.

LAST WORDS

The time would come when curtains will fall,
Hopes will be dashed with crows on the call,
A moment when fate turns out clueless to rage,
Last words through the pain will flip off the page.

Days when darkness wallops the light,
When redemption is far off away from sight,
Who would be there to lead through the way?
What last words as hays would be made through the day?

Books would be closed when stories are done,
With nothing to read, disinterest is born,
The journey of a lifetime will one day spell end.
The last words created could be hard to defend.

No matter the rebuke, the reaper would come,
Silent up in waves with the impact of a bomb,

Tears would flow, but life must end,
The mumbles at last are for irons to bend.

Uncertain is the day frost will set in and blast,
When coldness is felt with flashes of the past,
Fruitless are trials when a journey is up,
Drained are the last words like coco in a cup.

Days when life ignites romance with death,
A soul is consumed for another at birth,
When gifts through these phenoms
Are traded for love,
Words are still much granted one last time to evolve.

Difference in existence is deduced by death,
No richness or poorness in the belly of the earth.
All would be there when the harvest was right,
All words should be cherished for the suddenness of flight.

YOU DON'T KNOW ME

Before you sink your fangs in my world and suck,
Before you plant dynamites
In my foundation of rock,
Remember one miss is enough for all to go wrong,
You don't know me, so please don't tag along.

Like lions don't stalk, unless you are sure,
So rich are hunters that have turned out so poor,
The preys you know not
Are threats with no bounds,
Unfortunate are predators that hear not the warning
sounds.

Judge not unless you have the facts,
Unhealthy it is, please just quit the acts,
Unknown is much you choose to have known.
Lives you scrutinize are not your own.

Mock is your game, but not with my name,
If it is mostly lies you've made up to frame,
Crucify me only when you see I'm game,
Being blind, you should quit and care for your lame.

My tears in life measures not to your jeers,
Easy, it is to sneer up with cheers,
Crab holes I've crept with scars not to forget,
Nothing for me to be scared of, except the cold hands of death.

Stalk me not unless you want me to strike,
My venom on impact is deadlier than a spike,
Unfortunate are ships so lost out at sea,
Be wary of your moves as long as you don't know me.

LET'S PRAY

Into something like our mother's to summon
The weight that easily beset us,
Chanting shadows into words,
Myriad warmth harvesting solace
From one another
Petitions ascending into deaf clouds.

Wounds barely heal but wax into candlelights
Moulded into pillars of scourge
Tongues & fierce drumbeats
Let's pray into something.

Like our monsters beaming blue into bloods
Singing phrases to rapture the church
But dead bodies couldn't speak a word,
Neath groans and gulf
Hope these lips can still pray

Into a fate clamor & hysterical unbelief.

AFRICA AT STAKE

Match up young soldiers
The hill lies in doom
Stand up, young warriors
Fight for your freedom.

Who can dance to rhythm of pain,
Injustice and corruption
People of Africa are searching for a shelter
In the pouring rain,
Africa is a fountain of bloodshed, hatred, and suffering.

Watch it young life
Will you make it tomorrow?
Picture it, young life
Is it coming with pain and sorrow?

Who can build his shelter in the raging storm?

Tell the children, the future of Africa,
Be not at calm.
Slumber not there's fire on top of the mountain
Let young people dance to the Melody of strain.

Pick yourself up juvenile,
The future is painted gray
Teenybopper, your tomorrow is vile
Jump start your mind and have a say.

We're the best features in tomorrow's world
And the old folks are just dancing for today
See thoroughly through with a clear mind
Before you nurse your future in sickbay.

Young life break the chains of mental slavery
The beacon of hope on the hill is slowly fading
Fight back. It's your own future at stake
Ignore not, voice out makes that risky

Africa is dying before our very eyes,
And we are watching it with the full beam
Mama Africa is shrieking louder
And her children are as foolish,
As the mad donkey to hear her voice in doom.

APRIL 14

My mother is a cell of three tongues;
Three dirges of sons as big tumult;
Big! for the milk of her wailing breasts.

We are the thumbs guilty of the prison
Of home we printed for; we cry our
Pains loudly much of the tribal war
We're stuck in strong.

The cow as our head of printed glee
Has turned a stun bull, dread rampaging;
He gores us sores wicked so much
Inside the change we clamored for.

We are entrapped so painfully.
We cry for freedom

WHEN I SHALL DIE

In a dark room with no way of escape, may I lie.
Right there, the mark of death
Shall be certified upon me.

When I shall die,
May I never be found to be buried,
On the floor, will I decay.
Right there, termites and rodents
Shall feed on my body unhurried.

When I shall die,
May I never remember to prepare,
So that, my death be poised as natural,
In my ignorance, I shall perish and fare.

May my spirit find rest in a place

Where there is unrest,
May the ground on which I shall lay, be cursed.
And may history never find my roots and cause.
May the ones who tormented me perish with no remedy.

When I shall die,
May I never be remembered,
For good, or for bad.
Stranded soul shall mine be.

Insignificant and unimpactful,
Unimportant and unworthiness,
Unidentified and uninterested,
Will be my watchwords in death.

When I shall be swallowed up in death,
Nobody will see the foam that clogs at my mouth,
No one will witness the pain of wiggling and writhing endlessly.
I shall be handled, thereby; carelessly.

The stench of my decayed body shall fill the room,
My spirit shall take guard of what is left; nothing!
I shall be rigid as a rock,
And void of life, as a statue.

When I shall die,
I shall be forsaken in this world,

As I have been long forsaken,

But, may I be accepted and embraced in the life beyond.

WOMAN OF ESSENCE

Give her sperm,
She will give you a child
Give her house,
She will give you a home
Give her hug,
She will embrace you with love
Share your pain,
She will encourage you to be strong
Make her a queen,
She will stand in the absence of the king

WHAT WAS MY CRIME?

At the early stage of life,
Two weeks before sunrise,
The dream I had
Was to be one of mankind
But you had me killed before time.
What was my crime?

What was my crime?
To be denied of antenatal
You consented to my demise
You watched with your eyes
As he held the knife,
And took away my life.

What was my crime?
To be murdered by your hands
What prompted you to deny?

You never dine with a man
But only had with him a night
You pierced my heart,
And deprived me of my Juvenile.

What was my crime?
To be banished from breathing land
And be sold to the dead clan
What was my crime?
To be orphaned to the other side
Foeticide is of vile.

Murder is a crime
Crime with a price.
Womb like yours otherwise
If given a second chance
I'll rather stay back
Then be found in the belly of a murderer.

CHAINED

The wisdom of age
Worthless to a slave
Darkness could testify
To the lightning from the sky.

Little do I know, as others knew
No sun shine no light
Just like previous times
As others saw, I could not see.

All I loved, I loved alone
With naked foot I danced to their tune
Dead as alive
More like a lifestyle.

As I did speak, only to break
Freedom is death, suicide is rare

Hades engulf
Innocent skin on earth.

When the rest of heaven was blue
Of a demon, in my view
From my childhood hour
No minute walk without a cry.

Every labor left me sober
Being born black
Bind me silver
And stole away my paradise.

FOUR LETTERED WORD

Word with feathers that do not fly
But travels across borders
It stings unnoticed, like honey bees
Weird as joy that leave sad at bliss.

But when Mama's warning instructs,
Beware of falling for the red word
Opposite of right for the young
Much alike to be wrong if hurt.

Is this word danger alike?
To be feared like the masquerade guards
Black and dark, like a devil in disguise
But when lost, hardly to be found.

It veils like the luminous dots in the dark sky
And swings like a rollercoaster

The four letter word
My consciousness it blurs
Like I'm so high.

It flagged with Knights
It gripped my hands
It held my heart
As it crossed my path.

DEAR VIRUS

Orchestrating with or without dagger
Whenever with whatever,
Making smiles purge salty saliva,
Invisible thief of a dove writer.

Beret with gaggling tune of doom
Whose joy transcend from hullabaloo
Only to leave the world on a shaking stool.

Falling from the stairs,
Only to see the world drowning
But when impossibility was possible,
Nobody saw the cloud falling.

I wish I could sing
To swing away
But your rhythms are jinx

That makes the strong lame
You made life equal within fellow beings
Leaving the groom in the grave
And the bride, with feverish bliss.

You're much of a queen
Of which your presence spite meaning
Noble demon of brutality
Tell us where you live
And I'll tell you when to visit

Even if the world never does without you
We can live never to live
When your drama is over,
Let us know when to start all over.

REVOLUTION OF THE POOR

The wind sprang up hot in North
Against the odds of the crazy world.
Violence was never my way
But true is my pain.

Politicians full of lies
My leaders are clowns.
The wealth of many
Only to be shared in their cabins.

Those beautiful eyes that dreamt beautiful dreams,
Found are they struggling with living,
The misty eyes that pledged to the stars to shine
Wondering about seeking for better life with their suits and ties.

Fast the message went wide on the headlines

After collecting our last dines,
Education alone not a means of survival
Yet they live in paradise
With the same compass which took them to limelight.

Our kinsmen bombed
For their game of thought.
Divergence of law
For the benefit of their sons.

My cry, they tagged revolution,
Left they are in illusion
With hundreds of soldiers,
Fear still held them hostage like prey to the hunter.

Karma, not war,
The poor are fed up
The night is near
Vengeance is here.

IDENTITY

The epitome of artistry slam
An utter stranger of no land
Masked with elegant robes and rubies
Masquerading the floors of the hobbit.

My Culture;
Quintessential in color,
Like the smile of a mother to her son
Didactically vultures in an acrobatic form.

Dance if you can dance
Her beat drum chants:
If you ask me that,
Guided I am by her custom guards.

When praises go beyond,
Signal she draws

With her tainted crayon,
Don't be lost.

In the presence of an Oracle,
A child's head bend not
Beneath the cloudy drops,
Its heritage never fades off.

FATHER

Let me write about a man
A man known as father to us
A rankless soldier like an armed force general
In the absence of mama
Fed and changed our diaper
Glued our hands broken jar
Told us stories in the backyard.

Taught us love instead of hate
Praying with us part of his way
His presence with us always grace
Rather starve to lay
Then watch us sleep in disarray.

Toys and gifts, he had none as a kid
Day and night, he worked so hard for us to eat
Who's he?

The hunter of great meals
If not, the true great king.

The man of strength and steel
A single him
Dare not any he
Nor kin
As kind as he's.

Fiery like a macho
Love engraved on him like a tattoo
A diner amidst his crew
Far beyond measure,
Cool, calm and cultured.

Gift to us his words
A growing vine in us
In the heart of him above all
We were greatly nurtured,
To be reborn as one.

IN YOUR HONOR

Dear gallant fallen martyr
The slayer of beasts and giants
You were a hero in the legion
Striking up and down with the battalion
Until death from the sky,
Claimed your beautiful life as tithe
Of the tremendous victory won in the past
You left me cold with an armor
Like a soldier, stripped out of camo

Should I bow at the feet of your mother?
And tell her you died a gallant soldier
Should I tell your wife?
You died protecting your country and not her
Should I tell your kids?
There will be no father to cater for their needs
Should I tell your nation?

A gallant soldier fell today,
And there will be no more war again.

If ever called upon again
Would you rise up from the grave?
To be my right hand in combat
If resurrection is possible,
Would you join your beloved brothers?
To feast on the jungle leaves
And drink the moldy wine of the streams
That differentiate us from ordinary beings
Our elixir of immortality.

Could you please rise!
Arise in spirit
And reload my rifle with some cartridge
For me to triumph with your zeal
Taking down a hundred beasts
With a string,
Arise as I cock and shoot the sky birds for you
A farewell gallantry salute
For your journey home.

NELSON MANDELA

In you were we clothed
As your belly shield us from evils
Of life and its host
Just as the sky birth the sun, rain and the snow
You welcomed aliens into the world,
They never know
With your painful groan,
Damask with cold rose
Many would have considered as low blow
By the goal post,
But you breathed in just to leave the atmosphere with a
melodious solo.

Your words periwinkles on the saucer
Riddled with moral
Even when the skies fed you with tears
And kept you as slave inside the cage of trauma

You still manage to offer your children
A cup full of water
You're worth calling "wura"
The treasurable stone superior than "fadaka".

Your unpolished vocal lullabies the ears
Chasing away fears
Right in the moment of despair,
One to ten is the digits of the learned
But your bright tender care
Makes us indifferent to the alphabet,
Of the rich and their wealth.

A Shepherd with a thousand eyes
Whose sheep are flocked like the giant stride
Your deodorant disarm the desert
Leaving it waxed
For our feet's to march out bright
With the rod by your side
The father of every African child.

GONE WERE THE DAYS

Gone were the days
The days long gone
The days with no hope of return
Where nursery rhymes were songs,
Of every late night.

Gone were the days
Castle were built in minutes
By the architect of our hearts
Clay on our foots with crafting hands.

Gone were the days
Lies were soothing stories to our ears
Leaving us wandering in wonderland
Dreaming dreams of stars every night

Gone were the days

Running legs were friends to cycling hands
In the race of who can best
And who wins first?

Gone were thc days
Wealth was just a name
In the garden, we now play
And not a levy to enjoy juvenile age.

YOU'RE JUST LIKE ME

You're just like me
I'm dark and you're white
We're brothers of the same kind
Hearts aren't made of gold nor silver.

You're just like me
Mama raised me with love
I fell in love, and I drown
Just like you did, but couldn't wake up.

You're just like me
I traverse the road less traveled with a concrete heart
But the flames of lust
Choked me up with a harlot smile.

You're just like me
Your tears speak of pain and vengeance

Little do I know of the gun
Until I triumphed over suicide.

You're just like me
I can be wrong many times
Without being looked upon with pleasant eyes
Just like you, I wasn't born a perfect man.

WHILE I AM ALIVE

While I am alive,
Wine with me In the dark of happiness
Betwixt the fortress of heaven and earth
Hold me closer to yourself
And walk me through incandescence.

While I am alive,
Save the tears
And love me
Before Everest,
Sing to me, dance to my rhythms
Like that of the lovebirds.

While I am alive,
Pluck the stars,If you can
And save the script
After my demise,

I might end in paradise.

While I am alive,
Echo sounds of affection
From candor to splendor,
Wrong my wrong
And revolve around my world
With the light of your words.

While I am alive,
Come scale the sky,
On a stage of cloud
Gift me some roses
And make me smile forever.

LET ME SPEAK

Hold not my tongue
And fault not my voice
Let me set the captives free
With my mouth unsealed.

Let me speak of the pregnant cloud,
That fell on us.
Hot ice that froze and heated our hearts
And made us slaves of our clan.

Let me speak of the deadly storm
That took from us our crops
And gifted us its guns
To make us think we are one.

Let me speak of the paradoxical thunder

That fed us strong to slumber
That judged wrong right in the courtyard
And made tongues war against each other.

Let mc speak of the staged war
By brothers of same color
That gave us life in the slum
And fed us cheese with worms.

Let me speak of liberal
The captive and the jailer
The twin born of same mother
But enemy of their father's land.

Let me speak of the rainbow deeds
By the witches and the wizards
Diana and the sea
Birds of a feather.

Let me speak of the slaves
The freed but still in chain
The healed still feeling pain
A day meal only by grace.

Let me speak of the tears
That tilled the sandy soil
Like the nomadic wind
The prodigal son of peace.

Let me speak of the truth
Let me speak of the lies
Let me speak of the clowns
That turned everything upside down.

TELL MY GOVERNMENT

Tell my government
To lend a heart, if not born with one
To see through the doors of many
Whose teeth are carved with pains,
Whose pains are wedged into trauma
Plonking down cries in silence.

Tell my government
Of our tears that can't bring back the dead
But can speak of their heinous crimes
With the verdict of karma,
And its injurious bite.

Tell my government
Of the war,
Reaching for their doors
Waiting for fate's blade

To deliver the last blow.

Tell my government
Of life and death,
In case they might have forgotten
They are not born immortals
And for every beginning, there must be an end.

AFRICA MY ORIGIN

Not by color, but by deeds
I spare not the rod to have my child trained
I speak not of hate
For the stillness of my soul
Lies within my values.

I may be a traveller
To the rest of the world
Black as black could be
I know not less about my traditions
I can jump like the Massai's in a strange land
For my culture is my identity.

Show me your maidens
And I will show you
The daughters of my mother
The truer definition of moral

Whose bodies are carrier of my heritage.

Before night falls in Soweto
I may think of leaving for Lesotho
Not everywhere is home
But Africa is my home.

FORPOH TEE: THE GREAT HUNTER

The hunter, with amusing banter,
His flute sound flanks
On hearing, leopards run
The jungle trembles as he breathes.

The brave;
Whose wild eyes terrify the wild,
The forest leaves, bows at his feet
As he walks bustling and rustling
With his loaded guns and bullets.

Merchant of hunting ground
Slayer of beasts and giants
Whose gun goads like the gods

His bravery strides with chants:
Equal to the gods

Except Eledumare,
The father of all.

As renowned as a precious stone
Daring to the jungle beasts
Alluring to the beautiful maidens.

I KNOW WHY THE POET DIED

I know why the poet died
He died of a poetical trauma
That had his inkpot murdered
Within the narrow hall,
Of a poetic wall.

I know why the poet died
He died of an agony that leprous his soul,
A disheartening low blow against the growth
Of the memoir he wrote.

I know why the poet died
He died of a rebel against his pen
In the ocean of salt, he fell
They tongued and spited words,
Of hell in pretence
For the language of his is not of them,

That saw the blue sky as red.

I know why the poet died
He died of mixed feelings
Wined with asthmatic catastrophe
Aftermath of the scotch peels
Of visible resentment and envies.

MY MOTHER, MY AMAZON

While I whimper in fear and anxiety,
You were always there,
Like the moon in the night sky
While I whined and grinned at darkness pangs,
You shone like the stars and lighten my dark.

Without you, I wouldn't be, mom
And if I'd be, I won't be me.
For I can only be me if I passed through your gates
And yeah, you made me, me
When you showed me to the world.

You watched me grow,
Like a beautiful flower tender,
You showered love from your bosoms,
And all your care render

You let me drink from the fountains of your motherhood
as a toddler
And I grew to be among my peers, stronger.

Your face, though wrinkled,
Reminds me of the warrior woman that you are
My lioness and the strength of her king
You fought to protect your small little kingdom
And now your cubs roar and you smile,
Cause you hear in their roar your voice.

My Mother, My Amazon
A winepress of the choicest grapes
How so much yourself, you squeezed,
That our tongues might have a good taste,
Of your savoury
And even beyond your womb,
You've proved to be a mother to all.

RAIN RAIN COME AGAIN

For days beyond weeks, we had been waiting
With sweat infested skin, we breathed slowly,
Saving the little of the last breath left in us
We wore our dust tainted hair,
Kinkily clinging on our heads
Though we waited, it never rained.

Though our eyes were optically impaired,
We gazed to far distances
Hoping to see a thick dark cloud from beyond,
Yet still vapor kept on glaringly
Ascending in nearby fields
Not having pitty on the ashy,
Dry texture of my hands,
Nor the hopeless looks on many faces
Yet still there was no sign of any rain.

Rumors of its arrival had made rounds
From hut to hut, it had flared uncontrollably,
Agitating the eagerness in all of us
And for once, all the tribes were in one accord
We quickly forgot all the laid boundaries
What divided us had vanished
But as much as we needed it,
No rain seemed to be near.

All day long, we carried our beliefs with us
Hoping that faith would heal us
And uplift our spirits
A trying moment for all beliefs and deities
Quietly and hastily, I felt the meditations of many
But we waited and waited but it did not rain.

THE ROAD TO MY HOUSE

The road to my house is not a road proper
For the road to my house is a deformed
Stretch of land;
Strewn with rivulets, bumps, mounds, hills,
Lakes, and incipient gullies.
Incredible, is the state of the road to my house
It is like a smorgasbord of geographic landforms.

The road to my house impedes motion
It imposes a code for movement on people -
Allowing for side-to-side swaying of the body,
Along the lie of its contours.
It gives rise, too, to swift jumps,
Sliding and skipping;
Shifting and shuffling with unsteady feet
Along its pathways.

Falls are not infrequent on the road to my house
Falls from cars, motorcycles and the like occur
And falls from people, too
My own fall caused injury to my hip
And a stay for days in bed in pain.

The story of the road to my house is unpalatable
When it rains upon the road,
It seems the dodgy devil is in town
And the road becomes a soggy, slippery challenge.

Self-help has not helped the road to my house
This we've done these years.
We now wait, in hope,
Upon the coming of divine powers
To bring relief to the road to my house.

AND THE DRUMMERS CAME

And the drummers came with their drums,
A long time ago they came from distant lands.
And they arrived upon our shores
Their drums, with drumbeats, strange, yet overpowering.

Soon, the drumbeats sounded far across our land
And we began to dance to new rhythms,
And the drummers became our new dance masters;

Setting the pace for us to follow
As we danced in foreign ways -
Waltzing away on borrowed steps
Choreographed in distant lands
Our movements stripped of our culture, our tradition.

Then it was time for the drummers to go

And the drummers left
But their drumbeats remain with us
Our culture, our tradition, fighting for survival

SOLITUDE

I feel like staring at the beautiful rising moon,
To keep away the worries that come in noon,
Watching the flying bird makes me smile.
All to forget the sad memories being piled.

I stepped on the ladder to climb the trees.
To find peace, and for sadness to freeze,
There is solace in being solitary,
Whenever I sit on the lone tree.

I want the past itself to part,
And I wish the memories not to last,
Want a bright future to come,
So, I could use this present to perform.

I want the life of mine to calm my mind,

To open my eyes wide, not to blind,
I want my life to enjoy my deeds of my soul
So as to reap all the fruits of seeds, I sowed.

EVEN THE...

Even the stars can testify,
How your face calls upon,
The bliss that I can't rectify,
Through an illuminate beacon.

Even the moon can say,
How your love call upon the peace
That I'm searching for over one thousand days,
When I get no hope and when my heart also pierces.

Even the sun sees,
How my heart smile to have you.
How my mind feels the joy
Of your smile like a bee,
How my heartbeat keeps beating "I love you".

Even the night knows,

How I lie down on my diary,
And pen down the moment of no,
And in my dream you are the beauty gallery.

Even the day does wish,
To see your sumptuous face,
That makes you my everyday crush,
And your love passes through my heart pace.

Even my bed is expecting,
The day the stunning body
Will wish to use it for resting
And smell it aroma like candy.

Even my chair has fully prepared
The day the flat surface will sit on its surface
That is why it was quickly repaired
For the sumptuous crush not to sit in wrong place.

Even the spoon has cleaned itself
For the small buccal cavity to fill the being
Through the golden mold that was picked on the shelf
So the benefits are what it will bring.

Even the plate make, itself new
For the special visitor to use it
Without a single word, it already knew
That only the queen can use it to eat.

THE ALUMNI AIN'T THE SAME

Over some weeks, that bliss made me comfortable.
As the eyes of mine saw a gloomy angel,
It's suitable, not in taste but in blush
Because some eyes like her,
Just like I do, at the moment I met her,
She was a star.

The pot that was moulded in my heart
Can't hold the water anymore,
So, this made the feelings of mine to overflowed
As the water poured,
I moved close to her and told her how I felt.
Maybe she might consider,
It took me more than a month
For my mind to be golden pure.

She accepted my proposal
By saying "yes" was her answer,
I was perplexed and felt the pleasured in me,
Which makes me moved like a dancer,
As time goes, I called her every moment
To check on her due to my passion,
This wasn't my intention, but how I was pushed,
I couldn't mention.

To cut it short,
Her behaviour wasn't like how she was before,
I asked, orally and through indite
What has happened in fore,
She answered, I wasn't interested, but I accepted
Due to your wave towards me,
My body and it's system called the sadness
But not the tears as it hides like bee.

As guy, I kept it and continue our normal friend,
As soon as we finished the final exam,
She told me she loved me,
On the graduation day, I said,
Don't be facetious with me this time around,
I'm so serious this time
And don't get it twisted, she said.

All in vain, as the tears came out
From a strong guy that counselled,

When she said she loved her ex-
Much more and deeply,
I gained no conscious at the moment
And I couldn't say a word,
I wished I could go to the second space
And leave this world.

I considered all of them as a devil
That shouldn't be trusted,
I was confused and convinced by my friend
That they ain't the same,
She sighted my mom as an example,
But I say nothing once she mentioned my mum,
Because she is a good mother
I have never seen in this life of mine.

The dust dusted the sky,
And the sky scared the earth
With the thunder and storm,
The day I was given another chance
To have a rapour with a queen,
That accepted just like the other one,
But we moved on the boat with a sailor that sailed,
In between the tidy of the emotions of a low poorly guy.

We are in love and the love testified that
Alumni were different from one another,
Because the life as change and the happiness
Has cameo cane the wail,

The grounds why people wish us
Ecstatic companionship on earth,
Since we moved on the same beat and
Flow that flow and grow the aroma of flowers.

I AM NOW A PEN

I was born twice in a day.
I am now a pen
Dripping with thousands of inks.

My hand was injured
Where I bleed my thoughts,
Either when I am blue,
Happy or feeling red.

My brain sits in the wrist of my hand.
I won't be able to pen not until I use my hand.

I am a hero right from my birth,
I lay my feet on ground
And charge around the world.

Tomorrow will tell my story

Of what I have done yesterday,
And it will reveal the future.

The whole earth was awaken
The crown was born.
And the world can testify
When he follows not the gravity law.

Around the corner of my;
Brain, heart, mind, and soul
I rest the golden stylus.
Design with red like a vanilla.

www.ingramcontent.com/pod-product-compliance
Lightning Source LLC
LaVergne TN
LVHW010619100826
845148LV00014B/3029
* 9 7 8 1 7 3 5 5 4 3 7 6 5 *